ASTRONAUTS
and other
SPACE HEROES

FY! FOR YOUR INFORMATION

Smithsonian | Collins
An Imprint of HarperCollinsPublishers

Special thanks to **Roger Launius**, Historian, National Air and Space Museum, Smithsonian Institution, for his invaluable contribution to this book.

This book was created by **jacob packaged goods LLC** (www.jpgglobal.com):
Written by: Sarah L. Thomson
Creative: Ellen Jacob, Kirk Cheyfitz, Carolyn Jackson, Dawn Camner, Pamela Darcy, Traci Van Wagoner, Brenda Murray

All photos NASA except: **page 8:** APImages; **pages 8-9:** © David Hardy/Photo Researchers, Inc.; **page 9:** © Photo Researchers, Inc.; **pages 24–25:** APImages; **pages 32–33, all insets:** APImages; **pages 68–69, all:** APImages; **page 70, top:** APImages; **bottom:** © Mike Mills/Scaled Composites; **pages 70–71:** © Mike Mills/Scaled Composites.

The name of the Smithsonian, Smithsonian Institution and the sunburst logo are trademarks of the Smithsonian Institution.
Collins is an imprint of HarperCollins Publishers.

Library of Congress Cataloging-in-Publication Data
Astronauts and other space heroes FYI. — 1st ed.
p. cm.   Includes index.
ISBN-10: 0-06-089945-X (trade bdg.) — ISBN-13: 978-0-06-089945-5 (trade bdg.)
ISBN-10: 0-06-089944-1 (pbk.) — ISBN-13: 978-0-06-089944-8 (pbk.)
1. Astronauts—Biography—Juvenile literature. I. Title.
TL789.85.A1A875 2007   2006029755   629.450092'2—dc22

1 2 3 4 5 6 7 8 9 10
❖
First Edition

SMITHSONIAN MISSION STATEMENT

For more than 160 years, the Smithsonian has remained true to its mission, "the increase and diffusion of knowledge." Today the Smithsonian is not only the world's largest provider of museum experiences supported by authoritative scholarship in science, history, and the arts but also an international leader in scientific research and exploration. The Smithsonian offers the world a picture of America, and America a picture of the world.

Contents

Buzz Aldrin stands on the moon next to a scientific instrument during the *Apollo 11* mission.

Blast Off!

Human beings have always been explorers, wondering what lies beyond the next ridge of mountains or around the next curve of the river. We have always wanted to go just a little farther, to see just a little more.

And we haven't been content to explore our own small planet. We've looked up at the stars and the other planets, glowing spots of light that seemed to move in graceful patterns. We gave them names, told stories about them, and wondered what they were like. We dreamed of traveling beyond the sky.

In the twentieth century, we began to take our first steps away from Earth into the universe that surrounds us. In this book, you'll read the stories of some people and animals that helped us get there. Not all of them traveled into outer space, but they were all explorers—finding new places, discovering new ideas, and taking people beyond old boundaries. They gave us new ways to look at the planet we live on and the vast universe we live in, a space huge beyond our understanding, waiting to be explored.

Jules Verne

When Jules Verne announced that he was going to stop studying law and start writing books and plays, his father cut off the money he had been sending. Needing to make his own living, Verne became one of the first to write science fiction. He studied geology, astronomy, and engineering and dreamed up technology no one had yet imagined: submarines, television, spaceships. Before any of these things were invented in real life, they existed in the pages of Jules Verne's books.

More than a hundred years before the first moon landing, Verne wrote about a club of Civil War veterans who construct a giant cannon to shoot a man to the moon. His space explorers set up their launch site on the eastern coast of Florida—the same area from which the United States launched the rockets that sent astronauts to the moon.

At the Same Time
In 1865, the American Civil War ended.

H. G. Wells

Herbert George Wells's most famous novel is also his most frightening. In *The War of the Worlds*, Wells imagined Martians attacking Earth. No one can stop their deadly weapons. *The War of the Worlds* is such a scary story that when it was made into a radio play, people who heard the broadcast believed Martians actually were invading Earth.

Jules Verne and H. G. Wells were not astronauts, pilots, or scientists. But they opened people's minds to the ideas of spaceflight and life beyond Earth.

From *The War of the Worlds*

Across the gulf of space, minds that are to our minds as ours are to those of the beasts that perish, intellects vast and cool and unsympathetic, regarded this earth with envious eyes, and slowly and surely drew their plans against us.

Time Line

1828: Jules Verne born in Nantes, France

1865: Verne publishes *From the Earth to the Moon*

1866: H. G. Wells born in Bromley, Kent, England

1873: Verne publishes *Around the World in Eighty Days*

1895: Wells publishes *The Time Machine*

1898: Wells publishes *The War of the Worlds*

1905: Verne dies in Amiens, France

1938: In the United States, *The War of the Worlds* radio broadcast by Orson Welles (no relation) panics listeners

1946: Wells dies in London, England

A Martian war machine attacks a ship in this illustration of a scene from *The War of the Worlds*.

Robert Goddard

Dr. Robert Goddard poses just before launching the first liquid-fueled rocket in 1926.

Robert Goddard liked science fiction. (He was especially fond of *The War of the Worlds*.) He started thinking about the first problem that must be solved in order to reach outer space: how to build a vehicle powerful enough to get there. In 1919 Goddard wrote a scholarly paper claiming that a rocket could reach the moon. Many people laughed at the idea of rockets having any practical use beyond fireworks displays.

However, Goddard continued experimenting with rockets. He was the first to fly a rocket that used liquid fuel—the kind of fuel that would be needed to get a rocket into outer space. In his first successful test, his rocket went up 41 feet, not exactly high enough to reach the moon. But it was a beginning.

Wernher von Braun

By the time Wernher von Braun was 20, he had become chief engineer of rocket development for the German army. Von Braun created weapons for the Nazis to use in World War II, including the V-2 rocket, which could send a bomb to a target 500 miles away. The V-2s were built by prisoners from **concentration camps**, who were starved and abused. Many of them died.

After the Germans lost World War II, von Braun surrendered to the United States and began to build ballistic missiles for the U.S. Army. But his real interest had always been space travel. After the National Aeronautics and Space Administration (NASA) was created with a mission to explore space, von Braun became the first director of the Marshall Space Flight Center in Huntsville, Alabama, when it became a part of NASA in 1960. He helped create the Saturn rockets that would put the first humans on the moon.

Dr. von Braun holds a model of the V-2 rocket.

Dr. von Braun (center) explains the Saturn Launch System to President John F. Kennedy (right) as NASA Associate Deputy Administrator Robert Seamans listens.

Time Line

1882: Robert Goddard born in Worcester, Massachusetts

1912: Wernher von Braun born in Wirsitz, Germany (now Wyrzysk, Poland)

1919: Goddard publishes "A Method of Reaching Extreme Altitudes," claiming it would be possible to launch a rocket to the moon

1926: Goddard launches his first liquid-fueled rocket

1942: First launch of von Braun's V-2 rocket

1945: Goddard dies; von Braun and 500 other German scientists surrender to the United States

1958: The first U.S. orbital satellite, *Explorer 1*, is launched on von Braun's Juno missile

1959: Goddard is honored with the **Congressional Gold Medal**

1977: Von Braun dies in Alexandria, Virginia

At the Same Time
In 1960, when Wernher von Braun was made director of the Marshall Space Flight Center, the Beatles became a band.

SMITHSONIAN LINK
To see photos of Robert Goddard and his 1926 rocket, try this site:
http://www.nasm.si.edu/research/dsh/artifacts/rm-rhg1926.htm

The first living things to leave planet Earth weren't people. Before humans could travel into space, scientists needed to know how living creatures would react to the strange environment. To find the answer, scientists turned to animals.

In 1948, the United States used a V-2 rocket to successfully launch a monkey, Albert II, 83 miles above Earth, making him the first primate astronaut. (Albert II died in the crash after the parachute system on his rocket failed as it came back down to Earth.) Other rockets carried mice, rats, rabbits, and dogs into space.

SMITHSONIAN LINK
Animals as small as spiders have traveled into space.
http://www.smithsonianeducation.org/students/secrets_of_the_smithsonian/spiders_in_space.html

Time Line

1957: Sputnik 1 and 2 launched

1958: Explorer 1 launched

1961: Ham launched in Mercury capsule

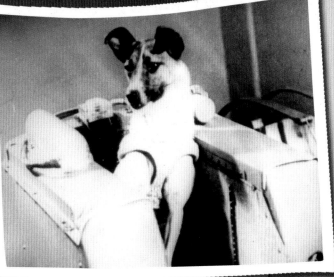

Laika

In 1957, the **Soviet Union** launched *Sputnik*, the first artificial **satellite** to **orbit** Earth. For the first time, an object made by human beings had joined the planets, meteorites, and comets circling in outer space.

But this wasn't the only surprise the Soviet Union had for the rest of the world. A month later, *Sputnik 2* was launched, and this time it had a passenger. Laika the dog, a stray, was probably part husky. She survived the first days of her flight but suffocated when her small capsule overheated and its air ran out.

At the Same Time
In 1957, *Leave It to Beaver* was shown on TV for the first time.

Ham

The United States and the Soviet Union were enemies, and Americans didn't like to think that the Soviets had gotten ahead of them when it came to space.

A few months after the first *Sputnik* launch, the U.S. government launched *its* first satellite, *Explorer 1*. Three years later, Ham, a three-year-old male chimpanzee, became the first primate to orbit Earth. Ham traveled in a Mercury capsule, the spacecraft designed to carry the first astronauts into space. If he survived, the designers would know that the capsule was safe for a person.

Ham lived through the flight, even though the Mercury capsule lost its air through a vent that opened accidentally. His space suit gave him air to breathe and kept him warm. When Ham made it safely back down to Earth, he got an apple and half an orange as a reward for his work.

At the Same Time
In 1961, the Berlin Wall was built, dividing East and West Berlin.

13

Guenter Wendt

Neil Armstrong once asked his fellow astronaut Pete Conrad how he got along so well with Guenter Wendt. Conrad grinned and said that it wasn't hard to get along with Guenter. "You just do whatever he says," he explained.

Guenter (also spelled Gunther) Wendt was born and educated in Germany. After coming to the United States, he became the pad leader for the Mercury, Gemini, and Apollo programs, responsible for preparing the spacecraft for launch. He described his job very simply: No one touched the spacecraft without his permission.

Wendt often gave funny gifts to the astronauts before their missions. (Neil Armstrong got a Styrofoam "key to the moon" before *Apollo 11* launched.) The astronauts gave Wendt something as well—the Silver Snoopy award. This award, a silver pin of Snoopy in a space suit, is given to someone who does an outstanding job, contributing to the success of a mission and the safety of the crew. In more than 30 years of working for the space program, Guenter Wendt certainly did that over and over again.

At the Same Time
In 1959, Alaska and Hawaii became the forty-ninth and fiftieth states.

Time Line
1923: Guenter Wendt born in Berlin, Germany

1942: Graduates from Beuth, Berlin, with a degree in mechanical engineering

1949: Comes to the United States

1955: Becomes a U.S. citizen

1959: Becomes pad leader for the Mercury, Gemini, and Apollo Programs

1989: Retires from the space Program

Guenter Wendt works with the *Apollo 11* capsule during a test.

Guenter Wendt (standing lower right) watches the *Gemini 5* crew walk to the launch pad.

What They Were There For

Guenter Wendt thought that Cape Canaveral, where he worked every day, was missing something: an American flag. Wendt believed a flag at the entrance would remind everyone who worked there to put a little extra effort into their day, since what they were doing would become a part of American history.

When he suggested a flag to the air force commander in charge of Cape Canaveral, he was told no. But Wendt didn't give up easily. He kept calling. He offered to get the company he worked for to pay for the flag. He said he would talk to people in Congress. And a few weeks later, a U.S. flag was flying over the south gate of Cape Canaveral.

Yuri Gagarin

At 21, Yuri (also spelled Yury) Gagarin was drafted into the Soviet Air Force, even though he was so short that he had to sit on a cushion to see out of his plane. Gagarin became one of 20 pilots chosen to train for the chance to fly into space. These pilots were given a new name—**cosmonauts**. *Cosmo* means "universe," and *naut* means "sailor," so cosmonauts were the sailors of outer space. And the first ships to take them there were the *Vostok* spacecraft. Cosmonauts could not steer the *Vostok* capsules; that was done from the ground. They were simply there for the ride—but what a ride!

At 9:07 A.M. on April 12, 1961, *Vostok 1* was launched, and Gagarin became the first person to orbit Earth. He landed 108 minutes later. During the flight, he was promoted from a lieutenant to a major.

Gagarin never traveled again into space. He became the director of the Cosmonaut Training Center, but he was killed not long after his thirty-fourth birthday when his MiG fighter plane crashed.

At the Same Time
In 1961, a first class U.S. stamp cost four cents.

Time Line

1934: Yuri Alekseyevich Gagarin born near Gzhatsk, Russia

1955: Drafted into the Soviet Air Force

1960: Chosen for cosmonaut training

1961: Flies in *Vostok 1*, becoming the first person in space

1968: Dies in a crash of his MiG fighter plane

Vostok 1

"Here we go!" Gagarin said as *Vostok 1* lifted off. He watched the continents, islands, and rivers slide by as he orbited at 17,500 miles per hour. When he tried to write a report about what he was seeing and doing, his pencil floated away.

The *Vostok* spacecraft had two parts, a sphere where the pilot sat and a cone-shaped **service module**. The two sections were supposed to separate before *Vostok 1* reentered Earth's atmosphere. But something went wrong. Cables still connected the two sections when **reentry** started, causing *Vostok 1* to tumble crazily until the cables melted and snapped.

As planned, Gagarin parachuted out of the falling sphere. The first people to see him after he landed were a mother and her child, who stared at him bewildered. "I am one of yours, a Soviet," Gargarin reassured them. "I've come from outer space."

SMITHSONIAN LINK
Discover more about the space race between
the United States and the Soviet Union.
http://www.nasm.si.edu/exhibitions/gal114/gal114.htm

Drawings show how the Soviet rockets grew.

The Huntsville Times

Man Enters Space

'So Close, Yet So Far,' Sighs Cape
U.S. Had Hoped For Own Launch

Soviet Officer Orbits Globe In 5-Ton Ship
Maximum Height Reached Reported As 188 Miles

Hobbs Admits 1944 Slaying

To Keep Up, U.S.A. Must Run Like Hell'

Praise Is Heaped On Major Gagarin

'Worker' Stands By Story

First Man To Enter Space Is 27, Married, Father Of Two

Reds Deny Spacemen Have Died

Reds Win Running Lead In Race To Control Space

Yuri Gagarin's first flight was front-page news around the world.

R-7 (8K71) Test vehicle 1957

8K71PS Sputnik (PS) launcher 1957

8K72K Vostok (3KA) launcher 1960

11A57 Voskhod (3KV) launcher 1963

11A511 Soyuz (7K-OK) launcher 1966

49.3

44.418

38.36

34.22

29.167

Alan Shepard

When Alan Shepard was growing up, he rode his bicycle after school to a small airport. He cleaned the **hangars**, helped push the planes in and out, and dreamed about flying.

After serving in the navy during World War II, Shepard was one of the first seven men selected to train for the Mercury program. The six others were Scott Carpenter, L. Gordon Cooper, John Glenn, Virgil "Gus" Grissom, Wally Schirra, and Donald Slayton. They were called "the Mercury 7," America's first astronauts. *Astro* means stars; astronauts were the sailors to the stars.

About a month after Yuri Gagarin became the first human to orbit Earth, Shepard became the first American in space.

After that, an ear problem kept Shepard off spaceflights for 10 years. But after surgery corrected the problem, Shepard took his second flight. He commanded the *Apollo 14* mission and landed on the moon.

At the Same Time

In 1961, Roger Maris hit 61 home runs, passing Babe Ruth's record of 60.

The project Mercury astronauts

Time Line

1923: Alan Bartlett Shepard, Jr., born in East Derry, New Hampshire

1944: Graduates from the United States Naval Academy

1961: Flies on the Mercury-Redstone 3 mission, becoming the first American in space

1971: Commands the Apollo 14 mission, becoming the fifth person on the moon

1978: Receives the **Congressional Space Medal of Honor**

1998: Dies near Monterey, California

18

Mercury-Redstone 3, *Freedom 7*

On May 5, 1961, Shepard was getting restless. He'd been strapped into his couch in the *Freedom 7* capsule for four hours, while the crew tried to fix last-minute problems. Then he was told that there was one more problem with the rocket's fuel.

"Why don't you fix your little problem," he snapped, "and light this candle."

The countdown started again, and *Freedom 7* blasted off to 116 miles above the surface of Earth. Shepard didn't orbit Earth, but he was high enough to experience weightlessness. He couldn't float though, since he was tightly strapped into his seat. After 15 minutes and 22 seconds, the *Freedom 7* **splashed down** in the Atlantic Ocean. The first American in space was back on Earth.

John Glenn

John Glenn poses before his flight in space shuttle *Discovery*.

Alan Shepard (and after him Gus Grissom) traveled into space, but they did not orbit Earth. The first American to do that was John Glenn.

Glenn had flown combat missions in World War II and 63 in Korea, and later had become a test pilot. But in 1962, John Glenn would fly much faster than he ever had in a plane. His Mercury capsule, *Friendship 7*, would travel at 17,500 miles per hour in orbit around Earth.

Glenn left NASA before he could go on a second space mission. Years later he became a U.S. senator. But 36 years after his first flight, he went back into space. This time his mission was to help study the ways in which the human body can change in weightlessness—changes similar to those that occur as people grow older. Scientists hoped that studying an older astronaut would help them understand aging.

Mercury-Atlas 6, *Friendship 7*
STS-95, *Discovery*

John Glenn was 39 years old when he blasted off alone in *Friendship 7*. He was 77 when he took off in *Discovery* with six crewmates.

On *Friendship 7*, Glenn tried some simple experiments to see how his body responded to weightlessness. He tugged on a bungee cord to raise his heartbeat, shook his head to see if he got **space sick**, read an eye chart, and ate some applesauce from a tube to make sure he could swallow. On *Discovery*, the experiments of the effects of weightlessness were more complex. Glenn gave 10 samples of his blood and 16 of his urine, recorded his sleep patterns, and even swallowed a tiny radio transmitter to keep track of his body temperature.

SMITHSONIAN LINK
Check out these photos of John Glenn and the spacesuit he wore on the *Friendship 7* mission.
http://www.nasm.si.edu/research/dsh/artifacts/hs-john.htm

Space shuttle *Discovery* lifts off in 1998 for the mission called STS-95.

Time Line

1921: John Herschel Glenn, Jr., born in Cambridge, Ohio

1943: Graduates from the Naval Aviation Cadet Program and is commissioned in the Marine Corps

1962: Flies on the Mercury-Atlas 6 mission and becomes the first American to orbit Earth

1974: Elected to the U.S. Senate

1978: Receives the Congressional Space Medal of Honor

1998: Flies on the STS-95 *Discovery* mission and becomes the oldest person in space

Friendship 7 launches John Glenn into space.

At the Same Time
In 1962, the United States and the Soviet Union came close to war over the Cuban missile crisis.

The Mercury 13

Seven Mercury 13 members stand together in 1995: (from left) Gene Nora Stumbough, Wally Funk, Jerrie Cobb, Jerri Sloan, Sarah Gorelick, Myrtle Cagle, and Bernice Steadman.

The Mercury 7 astronauts all had many hours of experience flying high-performance aircraft. At the time, there was basically one place to get that kind of experience: as a pilot in the military. The military didn't accept women for pilot training, so women could not become astronauts. Some women thought that wasn't fair.

Jerrie Cobb was twelve the first time she flew a plane. After she'd grown up to be a pilot, a doctor named Randy Lovelace contacted her. He had designed tests to be sure the Mercury astronauts were healthy enough to go into space, and he asked if Cobb would take the same tests herself.

Cobb and twelve other women passed the same tests as the Mercury astronauts. They later became known as the Mercury 13.

The male Mercury astronauts had also taken tests to see how they would respond to the stress and isolation of spaceflight and how they would handle spacecraft. The Mercury 13 wanted to take those tests too. NASA refused.

Jerrie Cobb and another of the Mercury 13 spoke before a government committee, trying to convince it that NASA's rules were unfair. But the committee decided that nothing was wrong with NASA's rules. No American women went into space until 1983, 22 years after Alan Shepard blasted off in *Freedom 7*.

SMITHSONIAN LINK
Learn more about the Mercury 13 as well as other women who made a great impact on the history of flight and space travel.
http://www.nasm.si.edu/research/aero/women_aviators/womenavsp.htm

Astronaut Tests

The Mercury 13 went through the same tests that the Mercury 7 took. At that time, no one knew exactly what outer space would be like. So they tested for *everything*.

The Mercury 13 were strapped to tables that tilted this way and that to test their circulation. They rode stationary bicycles to test their strength and endurance. They went through a four-hour eye exam. Their blood, teeth, balance, and reflexes were checked. The tests went on for days. Two of the women had to quit their jobs so that they could participate. All 13 were proclaimed physically fit to be astronauts.

Jerrie Cobb performing a test in the altitude wind tunnel.

The Mercury 13

Rhea Hurrle Allison

Myrtle Cagle

Jerrie Cobb

Jan Dietrich

Marion Dietrich

Wally Funk

Sarah Gorelick

Janey Hart

Jean Hixson

Irene Leverton

Jerri Sloan

Bernice Steadman

Gene Nora Stumbough

Valentina Tereshkova

When Valentina Tereshkova was growing up, she was the only girl in her town who would jump off a high bridge into the river below. Her experience served her well when she parachuted out of her *Vostok 6* spacecraft and landed safely on the ground.

Valentina Tereshkova became the first woman in space at age 26.

After high school, Tereshkova went to work in a tire factory and took up a new hobby, parachute jumping. While working in a factory where cloth was made, she applied for cosmonaut training. She was accepted along with three other women. The four studied together, learning math, astronomy, biology—but not flying. Since cosmonauts did not fly the *Vostok* spacecraft themselves, it was not considered necessary to give the women pilot training.

On June 16, 1963, Tereshkova was launched in *Vostok 6* and became the first woman in outer space.

Tereshkova also served in the Supreme Soviet, the Soviet Union's general assembly. But she never went into space again.

At the Same Time

In 1963, Martin Luther King, Jr., delivered his "I have a dream" speech in Washington, D.C.

Time Line

1937: Valentina Vladimirovna Tereshkova born in Maslennikovo, Soviet Union

1959: Takes up parachute jumping as a hobby

1963: Becomes the first woman in space; receives the **Order of Lenin**

1962–1991: Serves in the Supreme Soviet

Vostok 6

Valentina Tereshkova's spacecraft, the *Vostok 6*, was shot into orbit as the *Vostok 5* was still circling Earth. The two ships came as close as three miles from each other.

Tereshkova spent three days in orbit and went around Earth 48 times, traveling more than a million miles. She parachuted safely to the ground after *Vostok 6* reentered Earth's atmosphere.

Many years after her flight, there were reports that she may have suffered badly from space sickness. There were also reports that she had panicked and that her flight was cut short.

But Tereshkova was still the first woman to travel into outer space. For 19 years, she was the only woman. The Soviet Union did not send another female cosmonaut into space until 1982, and the United States did not follow suit until a year later.

Valentina Tereshkova is seen in a television transmission from her spacecraft, *Vostok 6*.

The *Vostok 6* spacecraft carried a single crew member— Valentina Tereshkova.

Ed White

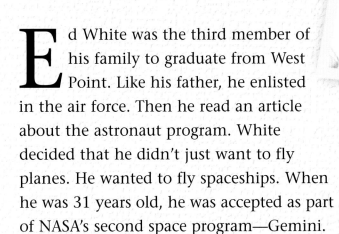

Astronaut White smiles just before the launch of *Gemini 4*.

E d White was the third member of his family to graduate from West Point. Like his father, he enlisted in the air force. Then he read an article about the astronaut program. White decided that he didn't just want to fly planes. He wanted to fly spaceships. When he was 31 years old, he was accepted as part of NASA's second space program—Gemini.

The Mercury program had sent astronauts into space one at a time. The Gemini program would send two astronauts up together. White was chosen for *Gemini 4*, along with James McDivitt. During the mission, White would make the first American space walk. (A Soviet cosmonaut, Alexei Leonov, had made the first space walk nearly three months earlier, but he almost didn't make it back into the ship.) During *Gemini 4*'s third orbit, Ed White became the first American to step outside an orbiting spaceship. Before Ed White could return to space he was killed, along with his crewmates Gus Grissom and Roger Chaffee, in a fire during a test of the *Apollo 1* spacecraft.

Gemini 4

As Ed White prepared for his space walk, he checked to be sure that he hadn't left the lens cap on the camera. Satisfied, he pulled himself out through the **hatch**.

Gemini 4 was moving faster than 17,500 miles per hour, but he could not feel the speed. Even though there was nothing holding him up, he didn't feel like he was falling.

Over his radio, White described his experience to McDivitt, NASA, and the listening world: "This is fun!"

White makes history by floating in space during the flight of *Gemini 4*.

Time Line

1930: Edward Higgins White II born in San Antonio, Texas

1959: Graduates from the University of Michigan with a degree in **aeronautical engineering**

1962: Selected for astronaut training

1965: Flies on *Gemini 4* and becomes the first American to perform a space walk

1967: Dies in a fire during a test of *Apollo 1*

1997: Awarded the Congressional Space Medal of Honor

At the Same Time
In 1965, the first U.S. combat troops arrived in Vietnam.

Gene Kranz

In 1972, Kranz (center) directs the liftoff of Apollo 17.

Mercury spacecraft had one astronaut on board. The Gemini missions had two, and the Apollo missions had three. Space shuttles can have a crew of seven or eight. But each time a spacecraft blasts off, there are many more people on the ground, working to make the flight a success. A lot of them are in **Mission Control.**

From the time a spacecraft is launched to the time the astronauts return to Earth, Mission Control manages what happens. The people who work there keep track of every movement of the spacecraft and every action of the astronauts. And if anything goes wrong, Mission Control has to figure out how to solve the problem.

Gene Kranz had been an air force pilot before going to work for NASA. Four years later he became a flight director, in charge of Mission Control. He led a team of controllers called the White Team and his wife, Marta, made him a beautiful white vest to wear to work on his first day. For each mission, she made him a new one. Kranz was a flight director for 19 years, and everyone became used to seeing Kranz running Mission Control in one of Marta's handmade vests.

At the Same Time
In 1964, Bob Dylan recorded the song "The Times, They Are A-Changin'."

Time Line

1933: Eugene F. Kranz born in Toledo, Ohio

1954: Graduates from Parks College with a degree in aeronautical engineering

1964: Becomes a flight director for NASA

1969: Is flight director for *Apollo 11*

1970: Is flight director for *Apollo 13*; receives the **Presidential Medal of Freedom** for his efforts in saving the *Apollo 13* crew

1983: Becomes director of mission operations for NASA

1994: Retires from NASA

Mission Control

Today between 15 and 20 people work in Mission Control. They are known as flight controllers, and each one is in charge of one particular part of a space mission. Some of their jobs are:

Electrical, environmental, and consumables manager: Responsible for the temperature, air, food, and water in the spacecraft

Flight activities officer: Responsible for planning and managing activities (like experiments) the astronauts do in space

Flight director: Leads the mission team

Flight dynamics officer: Plans and monitors the spacecraft's flight and landing

Spacecraft communicator, or CapCom: Communicates with the astronauts. An astronaut who is not flying the current mission is always responsible for this job.

Surgeon: Responsible for the astronauts' health

Flight Director Kranz worked here, in the Mission Operations Control Room at Mission Control.

Wally Schirra

Wally Schirra was the only astronaut to fly in all three of NASA's early programs: Mercury, Gemini, and Apollo. As a young man, Schirra attended the United States Naval Academy and was prepared to fight in World War II. But the war ended soon after his graduation. He stayed in the navy and became a pilot, flying 90 missions in the Korean War.

When Schirra was invited to apply for the astronaut program, he wasn't interested, but the more he thought about the idea, the more he liked it. He became one of the original Mercury 7.

Schirra flew on America's fifth manned spaceflight, *Mercury 8*. He also flew on *Gemini 6-A* and on the first manned Apollo mission. He has been around Earth 185 times.

Gemini 6-A lifts off.

At the Same Time
In 1968, Martin Luther King, Jr., was shot and killed.

Time Line

1923: Walter Marty Schirra, Jr., born in Hackensack, New Jersey

1945: Graduates from the United States Naval Academy

1962: Flies on Mercury-Atlas 8 mission

1965: Flies on Gemini 6-A mission

1968: Commands Apollo 7 mission

1969: Retires from navy and NASA

Schirra and his pilot, Thomas Stafford, suit up before *Gemini 6-A*.

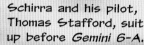

Schirra (center) was *Apollo 7*'s commander, flying with pilot Don Eisele (left) and lunar lander pilot Walter Cunningham.

Mercury-Atlas 8 (*Sigma 7*), *Gemini 6-A*, and *Apollo 7*

People called Mercury-Atlas 8 "a textbook flight." Schirra maneuvered his Mercury capsule on a six-orbit mission that lasted a little longer than nine hours. *Gemini 6-A*, Schirra's second mission, went equally well. For the first time, one spacecraft met another in space. This maneuver, called a **rendezvous,** was crucial preparation for the moon landing.

On the *Apollo 7* mission, Schirra and his crew practiced rendezvousing with a robotic craft and made the first television broadcast from space. The spacecraft performed well, but all three astronauts caught colds.

It's even worse to be sick in space than on the ground, since in zero gravity mucus can't drain out of the nose and sinuses. The only thing to do is to blow your nose—hard. The astronauts were supposed to wear their helmets during reentry, but if they did, they couldn't blow their noses. They refused to put on their helmets and made it down to Earth with no problems.

Gene Roddenberry

When Gene Roddenberry saw television for the first time, he decided that he wanted to write for it. He worked for the police department of Los Angeles, writing scripts on the side. Before long he became a full-time writer, creating scripts for shows like the police drama *Dragnet*.

Then Roddenbery had an idea for a science fiction series: *Star Trek*. The aliens in his show weren't the murderous invaders of *The War of the Worlds*. Instead, viewers met beings like the logical Mr. Spock, different but no better or worse than humans.

Star Trek was canceled after three years. But it stayed on TV in reruns and gathered more and more fans. Since then, there have been four other live-action *Star Trek* TV series, a cartoon series, and 10 movies. NASA even named its first space shuttle *Enterprise* after the beloved ship in Roddenberry's show.

At the Same Time
In 1966, Walt Disney died.

Roddenberry, shown here in 1987, imagined friendly aliens and humans exploring the universe.

SMITHSONIAN LINK
Check out this Smithsonian artifact—a prop used on *Star Trek*!
http://www.smithsonianlegacies.si.edu/objectdescription.cfm?id=263

Lt. Worf, a character in *Star Trek: The Next Generation*, is shown on the command deck of the *Enterprise*.

George Lucas

Lucas poses with one of the storm troopers from *Star Wars*.

When George Lucas was in high school, cars were all he cared about. He wanted to be a racecar driver or at least a mechanic. But after a serious car accident, he started to study harder, got into college, and took a class on moviemaking. Then he knew he'd found something he loved to do.

Lucas's third full-length film was *Star Wars*. He thought of the movie as a fairy tale, but instead of castles and dragons, there were spaceships, aliens, and swords made of light.

Star Wars won seven Academy awards and made Lucas a millionaire. Five more movies in the series followed. The final *Star Wars* movie, *Revenge of the Sith*, sold more tickets on its first day than any movie had ever done.

Television shows and movies like *Star Trek* and *Star Wars* helped keep people dreaming about the idea of space travel.

At the Same Time

In 1977, 15 countries, including the United States, signed an agreement to limit the spread of nuclear weapons.

Time Line

1921: Gene Roddenberry born in El Paso, Texas

1941: Roddenberry volunteers for the U.S. Army Air Corps

1944: George Lucas born in Modesto, California

1966–1969: Star Trek appears on television

1977: Star Wars: A New Hope

1979: Star Trek: The Motion Picture

1980: Star Wars: The Empire Strikes Back

1983: Star Wars: Return of the Jedi

1991: Roddenberry dies

1999: Star Wars: The Phantom Menace

2002: Star Wars: Attack of the Clones

2005: Star Wars: Revenge of the Sith

Moon Walkers

Buzz Aldrin walks on the moon on July 20, 1969. The lunar module can be seen in the reflection on his helmet's faceplate.

Buzz Aldrin

Buzz Aldrin's real name was Edwin, but his little sister called him "Buzzer," the closest she could get to "brother." The name got shortened to "Buzz" and stuck.

Aldrin joined the air force and flew combat missions in the Korean War. He'd heard about the astronaut program, but he didn't think it had much to do with him. A friend and fellow pilot Ed White changed his mind. When White mentioned that he planned to apply for astronaut training, Aldrin realized that astronauts were pilots just like Ed—and just like him.

The first time he applied to NASA, he was turned down. But the second time he made it. The man who hadn't been able to imagine himself as an astronaut was the second person to step on the moon.

Aldrin, lunar module pilot for *Apollo 11*, prepared to land on the moon.

Neil Armstrong

Before Neil Armstrong could drive a car, he worked nights in a bakery to earn money for flying lessons. He got his pilot's license on his sixteenth birthday. Armstrong flew combat missions for the navy in the Korean War and later became a test pilot with NASA. Over the years, he flew more than 200 types of aircraft, everything from jets to helicopters to **gliders**. He was selected for astronaut training when he was 32.

Armstrong commanded *Apollo 11*. He brought a small piece of the propeller from the Wright brothers' first airplane with him when he set out to become the first human to walk on the moon.

Armstrong manually guided the landing module during the *Apollo 11* mission.

Mike Collins

Mike Collins is the only one of the *Apollo 11* astronauts who never got to walk on the moon. But he did get closer to it than most people ever will.

Apollo 11 was Collins's second space-flight. "Here I am, a white male, age 38, height 5 feet 11 inches, weight 165 pounds, salary $17,000 **per annum**, resident of a Texas suburb, with black spots on my roses, state of mind unsettled, about to be shot off to the moon. Yes, to the moon," he wrote to himself during takeoff.

NASA offered Collins a chance to command *Apollo 17*. If he'd accepted he would have set foot on the moon at last. Instead, he decided to retire from NASA and become the director of the Smithsonian National Air and Space Museum in Washington, D.C.

Astronaut Mike Collins concentrates during centrifuge training.

At the Same Time
In 1969, *Sesame Street* was first shown on TV.

Time Line

1930: Edwin (Buzz) Eugene Aldrin born in Montclair, New Jersey; Neil Alden Armstrong born near Wapakoneta, Ohio; Michael Collins born in Rome, Italy

1949: Armstrong becomes a navy pilot

1951: Aldrin graduates from West Point and joins the air force

1952: Collins graduates from West Point and joins the air force

1966: Armstrong flies on the *Gemini 8* mission and performs the first docking in space; Aldrin performs three space walks during *Gemini 12* mission; Collins flies on *Gemini 10*

1969: Armstrong, Collins, and Aldrin fly on the *Apollo 11* mission, the first moon landing

1978: Armstrong receives the Congressional Space Medal of Honor

Apollo 11

On July 16, 1969, more than one million people gathered at Kennedy Space Center to watch as *Apollo 11* was carried away from Earth on a giant Saturn rocket. Four days later, *Apollo 11* arrived at the moon.

Mike Collins stayed in the **command module**, orbiting 14 times around the moon. Neil Armstrong and Buzz Aldrin flew down to the moon's surface in the **lunar module**, the *Eagle*. Immediately they could see that the spot they were supposed to land was too rocky. Armstrong hunted for a smooth spot. When he touched down, they had 20 seconds of fuel to spare.

Armstrong and Aldrin were the first human beings to leave their footprints in the soft, gray lunar dust. Armstrong had thought a lot about what to say. Finally he chose a simple sentence: "That's one small step for . . . man, one giant leap for mankind."

Armstrong and Aldrin collected rocks to bring back, performed a couple of experiments, and set up an American flag. They left a plaque on the moon's surface. It says:

HERE MEN FROM THE PLANET EARTH
FIRST SET FOOT UPON THE MOON
JULY 1969 A.D.
WE CAME IN PEACE FOR ALL MANKIND

Apollo 11 blasts off for the moon.

Pete Conrad

Everyone remembers Neil Armstrong, the first man to step onto the moon. Everyone remembers John Glenn, the first American in orbit. Not so many people remember Pete Conrad—except the people who worked with him. They remember Conrad's jokes.

All the astronaut candidates had to go through countless tests. There were medical tests to check out their health, vision, balance, and anything else the doctors could think of. They were whirled around in a centrifuge, a machine that creates pressure many times Earth's gravity. They had to master a machine called the MASTIF (multiple axis space test inertia facility). This metal cage spun in three directions at once. (Imagine doing a somersault, a cartwheel, and spinning like a top—at the same time.) It was supposed to feel like an out-of-control spaceship.

And there were the psychological tests. The astronauts answered question after question. During one test, Pete Conrad was shown a blank sheet of paper and asked to describe what he saw. Conrad stared at the paper, looked up at the scientist asking him the question, and protested, "It's upside down!"

Nobody liked telling the story better than Pete Conrad himself.

At the Same Time
In 1969, the Woodstock music festival was held in rural New York.

The *Apollo 12* crew included Conrad, the commander, Dick Gordon, spacecraft pilot, and Alan Bean, pilot of the lunar lander.

38

Pete Conrad, Alan Bean, and Dick Gordon, the *Apollo 12* crew, flew the second mission to the moon. Their Saturn rocket was struck by lightning during the launch, but no serious damage was done.

Conrad brought the lander down perfectly on the moon's surface even though the spacecraft kicked up so much dust that he couldn't see for the last few minutes of the descent.

Not a tall man, Conrad jumped from the bottom rung of the ladder to the ground. "Whoopee!" he said. "Man, that may have been a small one for Neil, but that's a long one for me."

Astronaut Bean climbs down the ladder of the lunar module to the moon's surface.

Time Line

1930: Charles (Pete) Conrad, Jr., born in Philadelphia, Pennsylvania

1953: Graduates from Princeton University with a degree in aeronautical engineering; goes into the navy

1965: Establishes a space endurance record in *Gemini 5*

1969: Commands *Apollo 12*, the second moon landing

1978: Receives the Congressional Space Medal of Honor

1999: Dies in Ojai, California, from injuries in a motorcycle accident

James Lovell

James Lovell checks part of his space suit while preparing to board the Apollo 13 spacecraft.

Maybe 13 really is an unlucky number. James Lovell had flown on three other missions for NASA, all without serious problem. But *Apollo 13* wasn't like that at all.

Lovell graduated from the United States Naval Academy and joined the navy, later spending four years as a test pilot. His fourth space mission was *Apollo 13*, which was supposed to land on the moon. But when an oxygen tank blew up, *Apollo 13* lost oxygen and electrical power. NASA and the crew had to work frantically to bring the crippled spaceship safely home.

Three years after *Apollo 13*, Lovell retired from the navy and from NASA.

At the Same Time
In 1970, four students at Kent State University in Ohio and another two at Jackson State University in Mississippi were shot during protests against the U.S. invasion of Cambodia.

SMITHSONIAN LINK
Check out this site to learn more about *Apollo 13*.
http://www.nasm.si.edu/collections/imagery/apollo/as13/a13.htm

The damaged *Apollo 13* spacecraft is hoisted onto the deck of a navy recovery ship after returning to Earth.

Time Line
1928: James Arthur Lovell, Jr., born in Cleveland, Ohio

1952: Graduates from the United States Naval Academy

1966: Commands Gemini 12

1968: Flies on the Apollo 8 mission, first to orbit the moon

1970: Commands Apollo 13

1995: Receives the Congressional Space Medal of Honor

40

Fred Haise (left), Jack Swigert, and James Lovell pose on the day before the *Apollo 13* launch, April 10, 1970. Swigert had just replaced Ken Mattingly as the command module pilot after Mattingly was exposed to German measles.

Apollo 13

James Lovell and Fred Haise were supposed to be the fifth and sixth men to walk on the moon.

But after *Apollo 13* had been traveling toward the moon for almost two days, one of the oxygen tanks in the command module blew up. The second was losing oxygen as well. The crew abandoned any idea of landing on the moon. They moved into the lunar module and stayed there as the *Apollo 13* limped back to Earth.

But the lunar module had only been meant to support two people for two days. Now it had to support three people for nearly four days. The astronauts shut down everything they could to save electricity. The lunar module became so cold it was hard for them to sleep. They could drink no more than one glass of water a day. Lovell was so dehydrated by the end of the flight that he had lost 14 pounds.

And since the astronauts could not fly the ship from the command module anymore, they needed a new flight plan. Normally it takes workers at NASA three months to write a flight plan. This time they did it in three days—but it worked. *Apollo 13* made it safely home.

With parachutes open, *Apollo 13* and her crew splash down in the South Pacific Ocean only four miles from the recovery ship.

John Young

Young jumps up from the moon's surface and salutes the American flag.

Time Line

1930: John W. Young born in San Francisco, California

1952: Graduates from Georgia Institute of Technology with a degree in aeronautical engineering

1965: Flies on the *Gemini 3*

1966: Commands the *Gemini 10*

1969: Orbits the moon in *Apollo 10*

1972: Lands on the moon in *Apollo 16*

1981: Commands STS-1, the first flight of the space shuttle; receives the Congressional Space Medal of Honor

2004: Retires from NASA

At the Same Time

In 1981, Sandra Day O'Connor became the first female justice on the Supreme Court.

By the time John Young retired from NASA in 2004, he'd worked there longer than any other astronaut.

Young joined the navy and served in the Korean War, later training as a pilot.

Young flew on his first mission, *Gemini 3*, three years after he'd been selected for astronaut training. He knew that his fellow astronaut Gus Grissom hated the freeze-dried food astronauts had to eat on their missions, so Young smuggled a corned-beef sandwich on board. NASA had worried about the bread crumbs that drifted around the cabin as Grissom munched, and sandwiches were off the menu for future spaceflights.

Young flew on a second Gemini flight, two Apollo missions, and the first flight of a space shuttle. He continued to work for NASA after his spaceflight days were over, as chief of the Astronaut Office among other duties, and retired at the age of 74.

This photograph, taken through *Gemini 3's* window just before take-off, shows Young strapped into his horizontal launch position.

STS-1—*Columbia*

Until the first flight of the space shuttle *Columbia*, all spacecraft in NASA's history had been used only once. Since spaceships are expensive to build, it would be better if one could be flown again and again. If *Columbia*'s first mission, commanded by John Young, went as planned, that problem could be solved.

Columbia blasted off from Earth like a rocket. In fact, it had **booster rockets** that provided extra power so it could escape the grip of Earth's gravity. Once these rockets fell away, *Columbia* orbited Earth on its own.

It didn't splash down in the ocean when its mission was over. Instead, it used its wings and glided down to land on a runway.

The mission was labeled STS-1. STS stands for space transportation system; all shuttle missions start with these letters. The 1 let people know that this was the first mission a space shuttle ever flew. There would be many more.

Sally Ride

When Sally Ride was growing up, Neil Armstrong and Buzz Aldrin were two of her heroes. Billie Jean King, the famous tennis player, was another.

Sally worked hard at her tennis game, and one day she met Billie Jean King herself, who told her she should think about playing tennis as a professional. Sally loved tennis—but she also loved math and science. In the end she decided that becoming a scientist would be a better career.

Sixteen years after Jerrie Cobb had protested that NASA's selection rules kept women from becoming astronauts, Sally Ride and five other women were chosen for astronaut training. When her training was over, Sally Ride became the first American woman to travel in space. She flew aboard the shuttle *Challenger*.

Ride had a second spaceflight and was scheduled for a third when the tragic destruction of *Challenger* halted all spaceflights for 30 months. Ride decided to leave NASA. She teaches physics at the University of California, San Diego, and has also founded a company to encourage girls to excel in science. Only one quarter of the people in science and engineering jobs are women. Ride is workng to change that.

Professor Ride teaches physics at the University of California at San Diego.

SMITHSONIAN LINK
To learn more about Sally Ride, the first American woman to travel in space, try this link:
http://www.nasm.si.edu/research/aero/women_aviators/sally_ride.htm

At the Same Time
In 1983, Martin Luther King Day became a holiday.

STS-7—*Challenger*

On June 18, 1983, a few minutes before seven in the morning, the space shuttle *Challenger* blasted off, and Sally Ride became the first American woman in space. STS-7's missions included releasing two satellites into space, one for Canada and one for Indonesia. One of Ride's jobs as a mission specialist was to use the RMS, or remote manipulator system. Basically, the RMS is a giant robotic arm with a joint in the middle like an elbow and another near the end like a wrist. Ride used it to release the satellites into space.

After 97 orbits and six days in space, Ride and her four fellow astronauts glided down to a safe landing.

Ride in the *Challenger*'s middeck wears a headset to communicate with fellow astronauts and people on Earth.

Astronaut Ride in space, on the flight deck of the space shuttle *Challenger*.

Time Line

1951: Sally K. Ride born in Los Angeles, California

1973: Graduates from Stanford University with degrees in physics and English

1978: Selected for astronaut training

1983: Becomes the first American woman in space on STS-7, *Challenger*

1984: Flies on STS-41-G, *Challenger* as a mission specialist

2001: Founds Sally Ride Science to help girls excel in science

Guion Bluford

Guion "Guy" Bluford told a high school counselor that he wanted a career in **aerospace engineering**—building spaceships. The counselor didn't think that was a very good idea. There were not many African-American scientists when Guy was growing up. And there were definitely no African-American astronauts.

Luckily, Bluford did not listen to his counselor. He did exactly what he told his counselor he wanted to do—went to college and studied aerospace engineering. And he joined the air force as well, flying combat missions in Vietnam.

When he was 35 years old, Bluford joined NASA as a mission specialist, a scientist who would carry out experiments in space. In 1983, on the space shuttle *Challenger*, Guion Bluford became the first African-American in space.

Bluford flew on three other shuttle missions for NASA before retiring to take a job at an engineering company.

STS-8—Challenger

STS-8 was not only the first mission for an African-American, it was also the first time the shuttle launched and landed at night. Everything went well, proving that the shuttle and its crew could work as efficiently during the night as during the day. Guion Bluford was responsible for some medical experiments and also for launching a communications satellite that belonged to the government of India.

President Ronald Reagan spoke to Bluford as the shuttle orbited Earth. "Guy, congratulations," he said. "You, I think, are paving the way for many others and you are making it plain that we are in an era of brotherhood here in our land, and you will serve as a role model for so many others and be so inspirational that I can't help but express my gratitude to you."

Bluford in 1992, a year before his retirement after 27 years of flying.

Time Line

1942: Guion S. Bluford, Jr., born in Philadelphia, Pennsylvania

1966: Becomes a U.S. Air Force pilot

1978: Receives a master's degree in aerospace engineering from the Air Force Institute of Technology

1983: Flies as a mission specialist on STS-8, *Challenger*

1985: Flies on STS-61-A, *Challenger*

1991: Flies on STS-39, *Discovery*

1993: Retires from NASA

At the Same Time

In 1983, the first music CDs were sold, replacing vinyl records.

Challenger
7

SMITHSONIAN LINK
To find out more about the tragedy of the *Challenger* and the brave
men and women on its crew, check out this Smithsonian site:
http://www.nasm.si.edu/exhibitions/gal114/spacerace/sec500/sec544.htm

Exploring space has always been risky. Before 1986, seven American astronauts died in the quest to explore space. On January 28, 1986, that number doubled.

Before the space shuttle program, all astronauts were primarily pilots. Their most important jobs were to fly spaceships. The shuttles have a commander and a pilot, and they also have five other crew members with different jobs. Many of them are mission specialists, scientists who are responsible for experiments. Other scientists, payload specialists, are sent by an organization outside NASA—maybe a university, research center, or another country—to handle a particular experiment. But no matter what her or his role on the flight, everyone on board a U.S. spaceship is called an astronaut.

On *Challenger*, for the first time, a teacher became an astronaut. Christa McAuliffe's job was to teach about the shuttle and the space program as children across the United States watched on television.

But none of the crew members on STS–51-L, *Challenger*, got the chance to complete their missions. A little more than a minute after liftoff, the shuttle broke apart in midair. All seven crew members were killed.

Time Line

1939: Francis R. Scobee born in Cle Elum, Washington

1944: Gregory B. Jarvis born in Detroit, Michigan

1945: Michael J. Smith born in Beaufort, North Carolina

1946: Ellison S. Onizuka born in Kealakekua, Kona, Hawaii

1948: Sharon Christa Corrigan (later McAuliffe) born in Boston, Massachusetts

1949: Judith A. Resnik born in Akron, Ohio

1950: Ronald E. McNair born in Lake City, South Carolina

1984: Ronald McNair flies as a mission specialist on STS–41-B; Francis Scobee pilots STS–41-C, *Challenger*; Judith Resnick flies as a mission specialist on STS–41-D

1985: Ellison Onizuka flies on STS–51-C

1986: Space shuttle *Challenger* breaks apart in midair, killing all seven crew members

2004: Each of the seven *Challenger* crew members awarded the Congressional Space Medal of Honor

STS–51-L, *Challenger*

It was January 28, 1986, a cold winter morning. The space shuttle *Challenger* blasted off at 11:38. Seventy-three seconds later, it broke apart in midair. Millions of people, including the astronauts' families and Christa McAuliffe's students, watched television helplessly as the crew cabin broke away from the rest of the shuttle and fell into the Atlantic Ocean, killing all seven astronauts. The disaster was caused by a problem with one of the shuttle's **rocket boosters**. NASA made no more shuttle flights for over two years while it studied the problem and made new designs to be sure that it would never happen again.

United States

Gregory Jarvis, *Payload Specialist*
Jarvis was a captain in the air force and a scientist who had studied electrical engineering. He loved being outdoors and liked to ride bikes, jog, and ski cross-country.

Sharon Christa Corrigan McAuliffe,
Payload Specialist and Teacher in Space
More than 11,000 people wanted to be the first teacher in space. Christa McAuliffe was the one chosen. She taught American history, English, and social studies in Concord, New Hampshire.

Ronald E. McNair, *Mission Specialist*
When Ron McNair flew on *Challenger* for the first time in 1983, he became the second African-American in space. A physicist, he also had a black belt in karate and loved to cook.

Ellison S. Onizuka, *Mission Specialist*
With his first spaceflight on the shuttle *Discovery* El Onizuka became the first Asian-American in space. He was a second lieutenant in the air force and a scientist who studied aerospace engineering.

Judith A. Resnik, *Mission Specialist*
Judy Resnik was in the same group of astronaut trainees as Sally Ride. She flew on the first mission of the space shuttle *Discovery*, becoming the second American woman in space. She was a scientist who studied electrical engineering, and she played the piano.

Francis R. Scobee, *Commander*
When Dick Scobee was growing up, he loved to go to the airport and watch planes take off and land. He enlisted in the air force after graduating from high school and served in the Vietnam War. He piloted the *Challenger* on his first mission into space.

Michael J. Smith, *Pilot*
Mike Smith graduated from the United States Naval Academy. He served in Vietnam and was both a test pilot and an instructor at the Naval Air Test Center. The *Challenger* mission was his first spaceflight.

Mae Jemison

Mae Jemison loved to read science fiction when she was growing up. But she noticed that the books she enjoyed rarely had characters who were women or whose skin was not white. The exception was the TV show *Star Trek*. Mae loved to watch the stories about the starship *Enterprise*, where the African lieutenant Uhura and the Asian Mr. Sulu worked alongside the Vulcan Mr. Spock.

Mae was 10 when she decided to be an astronaut. She began high school at age 12 and went to college when she was 16. Then she went to medical school to become a doctor, along the way learning to speak Swahili, Japanese, and Russian.

Jemison fulfilled the second part of her plan when she was accepted for astronaut training. She became the first woman of color to travel into space.

After retiring from NASA, Jemison created her own company to develop technology to help people in developing countries.

And she also appeared on *Star Trek: The Next Generation*. Maybe a young girl will be inspired by Mae Jemison's character, just as Mae was once inspired by Lieutenant Uhura.

Jemison posed in her launch entry suit (LES) before her first flight.

The *Endeavour* leaves Earth.

Time Line

1956: Mae C. Jemison born in Decatur, Alabama

1977: Graduates from Stanford University

1981: Graduates from Cornell University Medical School

1983–1985: Works as Area Peace Corps Medical Officer for Sierra Leone and Liberia

1992: Flies as a mission specialist on STS-47, becoming the first woman of color in space

1993: Retires from NASA

STS-47, Endeavour

The space shuttle *Endeavour* traveled around Earth 127 times on its eight-day voyage. As a mission specialist, Mae Jemison was responsible for the science experiments in the lab. She also investigated how **biofeedback** techniques might help reduce space sickness. In weightlessness, people may feel queasy or throw up. Biofeedback teaches people to concentrate on their breathing and heartbeat as a way to control nausea and dizziness.

Shuttle crews are busy while they're on board. There are many experiments to conduct, lists to check, tasks to finish. But Jemison took the time to watch Chicago, where she grew up, slowly move past as the *Endeavour* orbited Earth. In about five minutes, it moved from one horizon to another, and then it was gone.

At the Same Time

In 1992, President George H. W. Bush of the United States and President Yeltsin of Russia declared that the **Cold War** was over.

The *Endeavour* crew, shown in flight, included Jemison and Mamoru Mohri, an astronaut from Japan (far right).

Ellen Ochoa

Ellen Ochoa once said she loved being an astronaut because it meant she was always learning. On one mission, she might be studying Earth's atmosphere. The next, she might have to conduct experiments on what zero gravity does to human bones. There's always a new subject to study.

Ochoa got her passion for learning from her mother. A single parent of five children, Rosanne Ochoa earned a college degree one class at a time while raising her family. Ellen remembers how her mother always talked about whatever class she was taking and shared her new discoveries with her children.

Ellen Ochoa studied physics and electrical engineering in college, and when some of her friends applied to NASA to become astronauts, she realized that was something she wanted to do as well. A scientist who has patented three inventions, she was selected for astronaut training when she was 31. In 1993, she became the first Hispanic woman in space when she flew on STS-56, the space shuttle *Discovery*, for a nine-day mission. Now, having completed four missions, she has spent more than 900 hours in space.

Ochoa prepares for flight training with her helmet and breathing mask.

The *Discovery* launch lights up the sky.

Ochoa poses with her crew mates while in flight.

STS-56, *Discovery*

The crew of STS-56, aboard the space shuttle *Discovery*, was studying Earth and the sun, trying to understand how what happens on the sun changes Earth's weather. As a mission specialist, one of Ochoa's jobs was to use the remote manipulator system, a giant robotic arm, to release a satellite that would study the outer layers of the sun. Ochoa used the RMS to pick the satellite up again before the shuttle headed home.

One other activity Ochoa tried out on STS-56 was not part of her official duties. She brought along her flute to play for her fellow astronauts while orbiting Earth.

At the Same Time
In 1993, **apartheid** ended in South Africa.

From space, astronauts could see the delta of the Nile River.

Time Line
1958: Ellen Ochoa born in Los Angeles, California

1985: Graduates from Stanford University

1993: Flies on STS-56 as a mission specialist, becoming the first Hispanic woman in space

1994: Flies on STS-66

1999: Flies on STS-96, the first docking of the space shuttle with the International Space Station

2002: Flies on STS-110

Story Musgrave

For a teenager who preferred sneaking out the dormitory window at his boarding school to studying, Story Musgrave ended up spending a lot of his life in school.

Musgrave dropped out of high school at eighteen to join the marines, but after he left the armed forces, he went to college. By the time he was selected for astronaut training, he had five degrees. He later added one more, literature.

In his early years at NASA, Musgrave designed equipment for space walks, including space suits. He and a crewmate did the first space walk for the space shuttle program, using equipment Musgrave himself had helped to design. He became the only astronaut to have flown on all space shuttles, and his missions included one to repair the Hubble Space Telescope.

Time Line

1935: Story Musgrave born in Boston, Massachusetts

1953: Joins the Marine Corps

1959: Receives a degree in business administration and computer programming from the University of California at Los Angeles

1964: Receives a degree in medicine from Columbia University

1983: Flies on STS-6, space shuttle Challenger

1989: Flies on STS-33, space shuttle Discovery

1991: Flies on STS-44, space shuttle Atlantis

1992: Receives the NASA Distinguished Service Medal

1993: Flies on STS-61, space shuttle Endeavour, to repair the Hubble Space Telescope

1996: Flies on STS-80, space shuttle Columbia

1997: Retires from NASA

STS-61

Most telescopes look up at stars and planets through the thick layer of air surrounding Earth. This makes the images seen through those telescopes a little blurry. The Hubble Space Telescope was supposed to change that. Orbiting above Earth's atmosphere, it could take pictures in clear detail, and it could look deeper into the universe than any other telescope.

But when the Hubble sent its first pictures down to Earth, they were out of focus. One of Hubble's mirrors was a tiny bit flatter than it should have been. It needed to be fixed.

Three years later, Story Musgrave and six other astronauts repaired the orbiting telescope.

The crew had trained for over a year. In weightlessness and wearing bulky space suits, they knew that even the simplest movements—picking up a tool, turning a handle—could be difficult. They practiced until they were perfect.

Two months after the astronauts of STS-61 completed their mission, Hubble sent its first clear pictures back to Earth.

At the Same Time

In 1993, the movie *Jurassic Park* appeared in theaters.

Musgrave gets ready to be lifted to the top of Hubble.

Eileen Collins

Collins smiles confidently before commanding a five-day mission.

Sally Ride became the first female astronaut in 1983. The twenty-eighth female astronaut broke another barrier—she was the first woman to pilot a spaceship.

Growing up, Eileen Collins loved stories about famous women pilots like Amelia Earhart, the first woman to make a nonstop solo crossing of the Atlantic Ocean. Collins worked at a pizza restaurant to earn money for flying lessons. She joined the air force, just two years after women were first allowed to train as pilots, and was attending test pilot school when NASA selected her for astronaut training.

At 38, she became the first woman to pilot a spacecraft. (Valentina Tereshkova was technically the pilot of her *Vostok 6* craft, but, like all the *Vostok* spacecraft, it was controlled from the ground.) Later, Collins became the first woman to command a space mission. She said. "It is my hope that all children, boys and girls, will see this mission and be inspired to reach for their dreams, because dreams do come true!"

At the Same Time
In 1995, John Gray's *Men Are From Mars, Women Are From Venus* became the bestselling nonfiction book of the year.

SMITHSONIAN LINK
Check out these photos of Eileen Collins, the first woman to pilot a spacecraft.
http://cfa-www.harvard.edu/newtop/chandrapix.html

The space shuttle *Columbia* lifts off on mission STS-93 with Eileen Collins as the first woman commander.

STS-63, Discovery

On February 3, 1995, the space shuttle Discovery blasted off with a woman at the controls. Eileen Collins carried with her a scarf that had belonged to Amelia Earhart.

STS-63 was the first joint mission between the United States and Russia. Once enemies, now the two nations were cooperating to do scientific research in space. Part of Discovery's mission was to fly close enough to the Russian space station, Mir, to practice docking. (The actual first docking was saved for a later mission.) While Discovery was maneuvering close to Mir, one of the steering engines started to leak nitrogen. Collins worked to fix the problem, and NASA reassured the Russians that Discovery would not crash into Mir.

Eight days after Discovery had blasted off, Collins brought it down for a safe landing.

Time Line

1956: Eileen Marie Collins born in Elmira, New York

1978: Receives a bachelor's degree from Syracuse University in math and economics; begins pilot training for the U.S. Air Force

1995: Flies on STS-63, becoming the first woman to pilot the space shuttle

1997: Flies on STS-84

1999: Commands STS-93, becoming the first woman to command a space mission

2005: Flies on STS-114

The Russians

When STS-60, *Discovery*, launched on February 3, 1994, Krikalev was aboard, the first Russian to fly on an American space shuttle.

Sergei Krikalev

Sergei Krikalev wasn't sure he could be a cosmonaut. He knew that many people applied but only a few were chosen.

But he didn't give up hope of becoming a cosmonaut and was finally accepted for training. On his first spaceflight, Krikalev looked down at Earth from orbit and felt the way he felt when he left his hometown for the first time. He remembered how good it feels, when you're a stranger in a new town, to meet somebody from back home. In the loneliness of space, he thought, any person—from any town, any country, any culture—feels like a neighbor. The entire Earth becomes "back home." The man who wasn't sure he would ever become a cosmonaut spent more than a year in space.

Yuri Gidzenko

After Yuri Gidzenko graduated from military school, he served in the Soviet Air Force.

While still training to be a pilot, he dated a woman who would become his wife. When her future husband was just 19, she said to her mother, "You know, Mom, this boy can become a cosmonaut."

She was right. Gidzenko's first mission was a 180-day stay on the space station *Mir*, and his second was to travel to the International Space Station.

On missions to space stations, astronauts can spend months away from Earth. What's the best way to manage spending so long in such a strange environment? Gidzenko says it's fairly simple: a space traveler needs to do satisfying work, take enough time to rest, and remember that there are people on the ground who want to see you again as much as you want to see them.

Bill Shepherd

The International Space Station moves away from the shuttle.

Time Line

1949: William M. Shepherd born in Oak Ridge, Tennessee

1958: Sergei Konstantinovich Krikalev born in Leningrad, USSR (now St. Petersburg, Russia)

1962: Yuri Pavlovich Gidzenko born in Elanets, Nikolaev region, USSR

1991: Krikalev flies as flight engineer on Soyuz TM-12 mission

1992: Shepherd flies on STS-52

1998: Krikalev flies on STS-88, the first mission to begin assembling the International Space Station

2000: Gidzenko, Krikalev, and Shepherd fly on the Expedition 1 mission to the International Space Station

At the Same Time
In 2000, Charles Schulz, the creator of the *Peanuts* comic strip, died.

Most astronauts grow up dreaming about flight. Bill Shepherd grew up dreaming about boats. He went into the navy and became a **SEAL** and a scuba diver. He often thought that much of what he'd learned working underwater was similar to what astronauts learned to work in space. But since he wasn't a pilot, he couldn't be an astronaut—until the space shuttle came along.

The shuttle program was the first time people who weren't pilots could apply to be astronauts. The second time Shepherd applied for training, he got in. The sailor, diver, and SEAL was now an astronaut.

Shepherd thinks the space program is important, not just for the few people who get to fly into outer space but for everyone on Earth. People need challenges, he says, and the exploration of space gives us the chance to face difficult tasks and learn to master them.

Expedition 1

A spaceship travels into space and returns to Earth. The International Space Station will never come down to Earth. It was assembled piece by piece in space to be a place where astronauts can live and work for months, and it now orbits 260 miles above the planet.

People from 17 different nations helped to build the International Space Station, or ISS. The first piece was launched into orbit in 1998. Two years later, on October 31, 2000, the first crew arrived: Yuri Gidzenko, Sergei Krikalev, and Bill Shepherd.

The main task of the crew was to be sure that everything on the station worked. They turned on all the lights, made sure there was water, and looked through all the equipment.

They also had to exercise at least two hours a day. Muscles weaken in zero gravity. Exercising is an important way to keep them strong.

"What I want out of this flight," Shepherd said before he left Earth, "is for people to say that the first crew did a good job, and they came home safe, and they left, you know, a good ship in orbit."

John Herrington

John Herrington, a member of the Chickasaw nation, grew up when the Apollo spaceflights were capturing the imaginations of people everywhere. He often climbed into a cardboard box, lay on his back, and pretended that he was being shot to the moon.

As Herrington grew up, becoming an astronaut came to seem like nothing more than a daydream. In college, he began tutoring a retired navy pilot in math, and the man's stories inspired Herrington to try a career in the navy. After five years, he became a test pilot—and it occurred to him that his childhood dream might be possible after all. He was selected for astronaut training when he was 37 years old.

John Herrington became the first Native American in outer space. He carried something with him on his first mission to mark the historic moment: a blue flag with a picture of a warrior holding a bow, a shield, and a spear. It's the flag of the Chickasaw nation.

Time Line

1958: John Bennett Herrington born in Wetumka, Oklahoma

1983: Graduates with a degree in applied mathematics from the University of Colorado

1984: Joins the navy

1996: Selected for astronaut training

2002: Flies on STS-113, Endeavour

2005: Retires from NASA and the navy

STS-113, *Endeavour*

The crew of STS-113 worked on the space station, which was slowly being built in orbit. John Herrington and another astronaut did three space walks to install a narrow structure like a pole or a girder to carry power and electronic data. On Earth it would have weighed 14 tons.

Even though he had trained for a long time for this mission, Herrington said that it was difficult to get used to working in zero gravity. When you put something down on Earth, it stays put, he explained. It was hard to remember that in space, anything you put down simply floats away.

When Herrington took off his helmet and suit after, he became aware of a new smell. Other astronauts had noticed it before him. They say it smells a little bit like burned metal.

It's the smell of space.

Herrington walks to work on the space station.

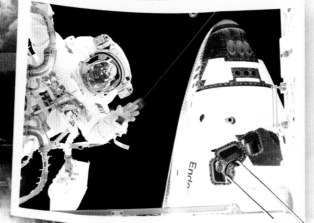

At the Same Time
In 2002, Sarah Hughes won the Olympic gold medal in women's figure skating, beating out Michelle Kwan (who took bronze).

Kalpana Chawla

Kalpana Chawla was born in northern India but left her native country to study in the United States. After working as a scientist for NASA, she was selected for astronaut training and became the first person born in India and the first Asian-American woman to travel into space.

Her first flight was on STS-87, aboard the space shuttle *Columbia*. The main mission was to study weightlessness and to observe the outer layers of the sun's atmosphere. Each time the shuttle passed over India, she pointed out New Delhi to her crewmates. "I lived near there," she told them.

Chawla flew on two more missions before being assigned to STS-107. On this mission, as *Columbia* was returning to Earth, it broke apart in midair. Kalpana Chawla and her six crewmates were killed.

At the Same Time
In 2003, the United States, Great Britain, and several other allies went to war with Iraq.

The seven-person crew posed shortly before their last flight.

Columbia's Crew

David Brown, mission specialist

Rick D. Husband, commander

Laurel B. Clark, mission specialist

Kalpana Chawla, mission specialist

Michael P. Anderson, payload commander

William C. McCool, pilot

Ilan Ramon, payload specialist

The *Columbia* mission STS-107's take-off led to a catastrophic reentry.

STS-107, *Columbia*

Columbia was coming home.

The crew had spent 16 days orbiting Earth. Now, on February 1, 2003, the ship was preparing to glide down for a landing.

As a shuttle moves down through Earth's atmosphere, it is traveling so fast that air rubbing against the outside of the space shuttle creates **friction**, and that generates heat—up to 3,000 degrees Fahrenheit. During liftoff, foam keeps the rocket booster from getting too hot. But when *Columbia* was launched, a piece of this foam had broken off and hit the shuttle's left wing. This damaged a panel that was also supposed to protect *Columbia* from heat. During reentry, the wing melted, causing *Columbia* to break up in mid-flight, 200,000 feet above the Earth.

All seven crew members on board died, the second shuttle crew lost on a NASA mission.

Time Line

1961: Kalpana (K.C.) Chawla born in Karnal, India

1982: Graduates from Punjab Engineering College with a degree in aeronautical engineering

1988: Graduates from the University of Colorado with a Ph.D. in aerospace engineering; goes to work for NASA's Ames Research Center

1997: Flies on STS-87

2003: Dies on STS-107

2004: Receives the Congressional Space Medal of Honor, along with the other Columbia astronauts

Technicians help Chawla prepare for her flight.

Yang Liwei

For the first 41 years of the space program, every person in space was sent there by the Soviet Union (later Russia) or the United States. (Most worked for their governments; two were tourists who paid to be taken on space-flights.) In 2003, however, the People's Republic of China launched its own manned spacecraft.

Yang Liwei became the first Chinese in space. He was chosen from 14 other astronauts in training to make the flight. An average student in school, he did best in science, and he joined the People's Liberation Army when he was 18. There he became a pilot and reached the rank of lieutenant colonel. Before his first trip into space, he spent more than 1,000 hours flying planes.

Yang said that his astronaut training was harder than anything he studied in college and more work than becoming a fighter pilot. But when he first got the chance to train on the actual spacecraft that would carry him into space, he was thrilled. "I couldn't help feeling excited," he said. "I decided that I must fly it."

At the Same Time
In 2003, *Harry Potter and the Order of the Phoenix* was published.

Yang Liwei flashes a victory sign after his first landing.

Time Line

1965: Yang Liwei born in Suizhong County, China

1987: Graduates from the Number 8 Aviation College of the People's Liberation Army; becomes a fighter pilot

1998: Selected for astronaut training

2003: Flies in the Shenzhou-5, becoming China's first astronaut

The *Shenzhou-5* landed in the grasslands of Inner Mongolia.

Shenzhou-5

On October 15, 2003, the People's Republic of China became the third country in the world to send a person into space. At 9:00 A.M., the *Shenzhou-5* blasted off from the Jiquan Satellite Launch Center. Orbiting Earth, Yang Liwei radioed down his first communication. It was simple: "I feel good—see you tomorrow."

All over China, television programs were interrupted to announce the successful launch. This was the first time many people had heard of Yang Liwei, the *Shenzhou-5*, or even the Chinese space program. The government had kept the launch secret in case something went wrong. Now, with everything going well, Yang Liwei was suddenly famous.

Twenty-one hours after launch, Yang came safely down to Earth.

Burt Rutan

In 1961, Yuri Gagarin became the first human being in space. Since then every astronaut who has explored space has been sent there by a national government. Only governments had enough money to build spaceships and train astronauts.

That changed in 2004.

In 2004, *SpaceShipOne*, built by a company created by Burt Rutan, became the first private spaceship to reach space. Rutan wants to take ordinary people, not just highly trained astronauts, into space. He thinks that ships like *SpaceShipOne* are the first step.

After serving in the U.S. Air Force and creating companies to build lightweight planes and experimental aircraft, Rutan secretly began developing the idea behind *SpaceShipOne* in 1996. Five years later, he was ready to start building his very own spacecraft. Shortly after *SpaceShipOne* reached outer space, Rutan announced that he and another businessperson were creating a plan to build a fleet of spaceships that will fly tourists into outer space.

SpaceShipOne glides to a landing at Mojave space port.

At the Same Time

In 2005, Hurricane Katrina caused terrible damage to New Orleans and the U.S. Gulf Coast.

Time Line

1943: Burt Rutan born in Portland, Oregon

1965: Graduates from California Polytechnic University with a degree in aeronautical engineering

1982: Founds Scaled Composites, the company that built *SpaceShipOne*

2004: *SpaceShipOne* wins the Ansari X Prize

2005: Founds the Spaceship Company to take tourists into space

WHITE KNIGHT

Small round windows give *White Knight*'s pilot a view of the horizon.

SpaceShipOne and White Knight

SpaceShipOne was built to compete for the Ansari X Prize: $10 million offered for the first vehicle *not* built by a national government that could reach suborbital space—a height of slightly more than 62 miles above Earth. Gravity is much weaker in suborbital space, so astronauts experience weightlessness, even though their ship is not traveling fast enough to orbit.

To win the prize, a ship had to reach suborbital space twice in two weeks. *SpaceShipOne*, piloted by Mike Melvill, soared up 64 miles above Earth on September 29, 2004. Five days later, it reached an altitude of 67 miles with pilot Brian Binnie at the controls.

SpaceShipOne is carried up to a height of about 47,000 feet by another aircraft, a jet named *White Knight*. *White Knight* releases *SpaceShipOne*, which takes off to soar up above Earth's atmosphere on its own power before gliding in for a landing.

Moon, Mars, and Beyond

Astronaut Gene Cernan goes for a drive on the moon.

NASA has new plans for exploring space. It hopes to send human beings back to the moon.

A new spaceship is being designed and built to take them there. This ship will look more like the Apollo rocket than the space shuttle, but it will be three times bigger, capable of carrying a crew of four. First, a heavy-lift rocket will blast into space, carrying a lunar lander. Then, with another rocket, the capsule carrying the crew will take off, dock with the lunar lander, and head for the moon.

Once in orbit around the moon, the crew will descend to the surface in the lander. At first the astronauts will stay four to seven days on the moon's surface. Later, NASA plans to build a **lunar outpost**, where crews can stay for up to six months. When they are ready to leave, the crew will use a part of the lander to blast up to the capsule, waiting for them in orbit. The capsule will take them back to Earth.

NASA hopes to use what the astronauts and scientists learn about traveling to the moon and living there when it comes time for a trip to Mars. Where might we go after Mars? The universe is bigger than we know, and we are just beginning to explore it. In less than half a century, human beings have taken their first steps into space. Where could we go in another 50 years? How far can you imagine?

SMITHSONIAN LINK
Visit the National Air and Space Museum home page
to find out the latest news in space exploration.
http://www.nasm.si.edu

Meet the Pad Leader

Wendt speaks after the *Liberty Bell 7* capsule is recovered.

Interview with Guenter Wendt

Why did you become an aeronautical engineer?

Even in grade school I was amazed at model airplanes. So I made my own. Later on I started to make gliders. At 14 years of age, I was one of the only boys who had a glider's license. I was fascinated with airplanes.

How can kids get interested in this field?

When I was little, I wanted to know how an alarm clock set off an alarm. So I opened it up and looked inside. Curiosity is what gets you going in what direction you want to go. When one of my cousins got an electric train for Christmas, I needed to find out how it was working.

You know, "Where does the power come from?" and things like that.

What did you do on an average day at Cape Canaveral?

Ha! Well, we had very few average days. I mean at Cape Canaveral, our average day was between 12 and 14 hours of work. And we worked six days a week.

What do you think would be the most surprising thing about your job to people who aren't involved in the space program?

The most surprising thing is that you can hardly believe you could accomplish all these things. For instance, when President Kennedy said, Okay, we are going to the moon! At that point in the game, we barely had looked at launching the first man into space! And we said, "Man, we don't know how we can do that!" But this is when you go ahead and start asking, okay, how do we do

Guenter Wendt (right) helps David Scott, commander of *Apollo 15*, with flight preparations.

that? And piece by piece—now you make mistakes, you have things that don't work out—but that's how you learn. As a matter of fact, one of my great teachers once said, when I had to admit to a mistake, "That is not a problem. A mistake means that you have been working on something. If you never make a mistake, you never work."

What was the most exciting moment during your work for the space program?

The most emotional one, actually, was Alan Shepard's launch, because it was our first man in space. Now at that time we were launching 15, 20 missiles a week. But three out of five would either blow up out over the ocean or just didn't go. But for Shepard's flight, we said, "Man, there is something in that rocket that you don't want to lose."

Did you ever want to go into space yourself?

I would have liked to, but I realized it took quite a bit more education and things like that that I hadn't had.

What do you think will happen to the space program in the future—where will astronauts go?

I think, to be very realistic, I believe they will go back to the moon, and I don't think that Mars is in my or in the next generation's lifetime. Because right now, maybe people are saying we are going to Mars, but we have no way, even conceivable, to protect the people from radiation. I say, "Okay, if we go to the moon, let's put an

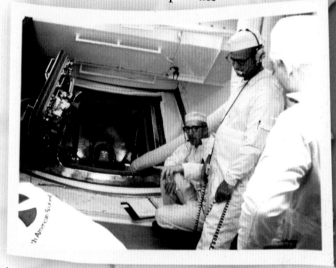

Wendt as pad leader, kneeling, helps *Apollo 11* astronauts prepare for flight.

atomic generating system on the moon and use lunar atomic fusion rather than fission, which does not have any by-products, you know, just water." As I talk to engineering students, I say that if they really want to make an impact on Earth and all the population, they need to invent a way to conduct electric power without wires. Because then we could generate power on the moon and just beam it down to Earth.

Glossary

aeronautics, aeronautical engineering—The science of the design and construction of aircraft.

aerospace engineering—The science of the design and construction of aircraft, missiles, and spacecraft.

apartheid—The former system of government in South Africa, where people were separated by race, and white people were privileged.

astronaut—The American name for space travelers.

biofeedback—A system of controlling breathing, heart rate, muscle tension, and other factors to help improve health.

booster rocket—A rocket that provides extra power to a spaceship when it launches; the booster then falls away from the spaceship.

Cold War—A phrase used to describe the relationship between the United States and the Soviet Union from after World War II until the Soviet Union came apart. The countries considered each other enemies but never actually went to war.

command module—The main control and human habitat of a spacecraft.

concentration camps—German prison camps where Jews, Gypsies, prisoners of war, and others were kept during World War II, often in terrible conditions.

Congressional Gold Medal—An award given to express national appreciation for distinguished achievements and contributions.

Congressional Space Medal of Honor—An award given for exceptional contributions to national welfare. Only astronauts can receive this medal.

cosmonauts—The Soviet name for astronauts.

friction—Resistance experienced by an object or surface when moving against another object or surface.

glider—A winged aircraft that has no engine.

hangar—A building where airplanes are kept.

hatch—An opening in a floor or a roof.

lunar module—The section of the Apollo spacecraft that separated from the command module to land on the moon.

lunar outpost—A proposed station on the moon.

Mission Control—The room where flight controllers and a flight director, working for NASA, oversee all aspects of a spaceflight from launch to landing.

orbit—To move around a center of gravity, such as a planet or a star.

Order of Lenin—The highest award given by the Soviet Union to both civilians and military personnel.

per annum—Each year.

Presidential Medal of Freedom—An award given for exceptional contributions to national security, world peace, culture, or public service; the highest award a U.S. civilian can receive.

reentry—The process by which a spacecraft leaves outer space and comes back into Earth's atmosphere.

rendezvous—Docking to objects in space (in the space program).

satellite—Anything that orbits around a center of gravity, such as a planet or a star.

SEAL—A member of a specialized, highly trained navy unit. SEAL stands for SEa, Air, and Land.

service module—The section of a spacecraft containing fuel, water, and the electrical and other systems necessary to run the spacecraft.

Soviet Union, or Union of Soviet Socialist Republics—The country created in 1922 when Russia joined with three other territories. The USSR was the first communist country and the largest country in the world. It broke up into separate, independent countries in 1991.

space sick—To become nauseous or queasy because of the disorientation of weightlessness.

splash down—To land in water rather than on land.

More to See and Read

WEBSITES

There are links to many wonderful web pages in this book. But the web is constantly growing and changing, so we cannot guarantee that the sites we recommend will be available. If the site you want is no longer there, you can always find your way to plenty of information about space exploration and a great learning experience through the main Smithsonian website: www.si.edu.

To find out more about how spaceships, space stations, and space suits work, try this site:
http://science.howstuffworks.com

To find out more about *SpaceShipOne* and see videos of its prize-winning flight, visit:
http://www.scaled.com/projects/tierone/index.htm

To read biographies of astronauts, go to:
http://www.jsc.nasa.gov/Bios

To learn more about the history of spaceflight and the Mercury, Gemini, and Apollo programs, try:
http://history.nasa.gov/tindex.html#5

To read more about the *Challenger* and *Columbia* shuttle disasters, see these sites:
http://history.nasa.gov/columbia
http://history.nasa.gov/sts51l.html
http://www.challenger.org/about/crew_bios.cfm

To read about women in the American space program, visit:
http://quest.arc.nasa.gov/women

SUGGESTED READING

Wings and Rockets: The Story of Women in Air and Space by Jeannine Atkins, illustrated by Dušan Petričič.

Black Stars in Orbit: NASA's African American Astronauts by Khephra Burns and William Miles.

Liftoff: The Story of America's Adventure in Space by Michael Collins, illustrated by James Dean.

Find Where the Wind Goes: Moments from My Life by Dr. Mae Jemison.

To Space and Back by Sally K. Ride with Susan Okie.

The Man Who Went to the Far Side of the Moon: The Story of Apollo 11 Astronaut Michael Collins by Bea Uusma Schyffert.

Index